the bare north:

poems from an outsider

Austin Campbell

BookLeaf
Publishing

India | USA | UK

the bare north: poems from an outsider

© 2021 Austin Campbell

Presentation by *BookLeaf Publishing*

Web: www.bookleafpub.com

E-mail: info@bookleafpub.com

ISBN : 9789358362336

First edition 2021

For Carlton.

Acknowledgement

Many thanks to the families who have shaped me, and to the people I have loved and lost.

1. migration

when the black pebbles

crept into the crevices

of my shoes

and pulled me deeper into

the earth

I felt connected -

like I feel with you;

i wanted to pick the flowers

and give them to you

but they'd never make it back

across the sea

of anxiety I skid.

There

I sunk:

into the sand,

out of luck,

dreaming of love,

sick with it to the bone–

infected,

I heard

glassy waves shattering cold

against shifting mossy rockfaces.

windblown waves,

how my heart

is full of the changing colours of our
souls;

the water transforms,

miles shallow

        before

              the riptide,

light

                 to dark

to light again...

        until

cool silence arrives;

             sweet music

      of a babbling beachfront,

         historic bedrock

and

the wreck of the edmund

fitzgerald

hidden beneath.

here I root

to begin my new life

at the

edge of the world.

2.knife's edge

seventy-five saturdays ago,

i wasn't here

in reality,

i didn't feel safe -

i still barely feel;

that old pair of red converse

worn through.

my soul,

burning down,

layersof

martyr memories:

my head is messy,

tired with voices,

unable to communicate.

why can't human beings live

in harmony with nature?

why can't i be at peace with myself?

                        somedays,

             they're the same question,

               double-edged swords

                    duelling

       for control of a shipwreck,

wild dogs playing tug-of-war,

       untili break -

                   i realize

            those wild dogs,

             remain at my

beck

      and

                  call

likethese words.

seventy-five saturdays ago,

every light flickered

andi can't remember

ifi held myself.

didi remind myself that it's okay

to love yourself

for as long as possible?

                        i stopped caring;

            too many fires and not enough

                              extinguishers,

and an abandoned building full of ghosts

                with a caretaker who retired

                            (see: escaped)

from that helpless service.

lastsaturday,

i landed here,

ship somehow intact,

locking eyes

with a Giant,

blessed with light

by the rising Sun;

i understand now:

souls stir,

dreams awaken

wheni do,

and

i lose so much of myself

on the regular.

i am safer than i was

yet

threats wander still in

dark spaces.

between the trees,

voices echo

from whisper to **thunder**

and

i hide

from everyone,

everything -

that which i am still trying to find:

myself.

soi keep the world quiet around me,

waiting for my own voice to join

a demanding chorus

without losing sight of myself…

the universe can take care of the rest.

3.Requiem

we tread

over the lines

we've drawn,

redrawn,

cut until

there is nothing left.

blood's in them hills

where it always is,

isn't it?

purity is a lie.

we all bleed

we all want

we all forget

colonization crushes countless souls

like

brick and glass,

an entire ten-story building

collapsing on top of you,

in repetition -

inflated insanity,

blown-up reality,

the weight

(more than a song or a prayer)

oh god:

a drunken, stupid, angry man

deserted by white prophets,

fills his glass with a fistful of drywall

and

one too many apologies

for wanton destruction

for gluttony, greed, and

who wrote the book on these sins,
anyway?

how did hatred become so calculated?

insidious indulgence;

making good on our insatiable need

to relive the past

to repeat human history

keep the fire burning so long that we are
all reduced to

ashes.

14

4.roadrunner

we were young

like love

when it dazzles

and makes you

sparkle

with electric defiance.

          teenagers trapped in adult lives.

        we are what they never told us we
                  would have to be.

the road stretched out,

     huggingAsaka's curves,

          while we sailed;

see, making waves is important work.

it'sall personal.

the light began to dim.

                    but friends,

        there is beauty to be found

in the twilight at dusk

when laughter prevails,

            where life simply happens.

leaves give way to snowflakes,

            snowflakes to rain,

rays of heat refresh it all

                    buti wish they wouldn't -

sometimes

remember:

soft blanket-cocoons

and scary movies

and marvel movies

                    iremember getting high

                    to forget how low i was

                    screaming inside my head

                    without uttering a word.

my mind runs

          like the road;

                    i'm drawn to it.

                    i love road trips

                    i love my friends

                    i love the feeling

the grasp of a steering wheel;

no chosen destination,

just driving

beyond city limits,

blasting music that frees the soul,

makes me feel

alive.

the road never really quite ends.

i never really quite want it to.

5.from red to blue

i've been trying to write pain

       into prose -

turn blood into wine

for you to digest

       all of these emotions i experience

       but

the bitter taste of alcohol

       overpowers sweetness,

       there is no resilience;

       my mind is past due:

sour grapes.

6. life: at what cost?

feel lost within' yourself -

left alone in self-containment,

the blood flecks the inner walls

and you see red;

shutting out other voices,

you fall far,

fast.

the self becomes as vast and terrifying
as outer space,

a cage becomes a spaceship;

oxygen depleting,

beating yourself into submission

awestruck by reality,

bloody-faced,

a self-made martyr

flooding the causeway without recourse
to part the tide...

no way to progress -

to shepherd yourself through the grim
darkness and uncertainty,

locked in:

depressed,

anxious,

lonely,

tired.

vandals of personalities past and
present

come to me for round one-two-three,

yet, wash away in the silt fragments

of time that elude me,

slip through the cracks in my brain and
disappear

do you let the shards of self-pity shatter
you?

let the tide close in on both sides and
consume you whole?

kill a mind that never learned to love
itself properly?

or write,

hang hope away from that

phantom pain,

biting cynicism,

bitten tongue,

and

burning trauma?

there is no answer given.

a bittersweet silence.

7.summer ITALIANO

i am sunk

shipwrecked

drowning

in

sweet sap;

bleeding heart:

i make messes

in my mind

and

scrape the dirt off my knees

afteri fall

becausei don't need filthy sheets,

left to collect the pieces

falling

i kiss you and it's like

i should have done that earlier

but time is measured by

moments we make

like the thoughts conjured

that make men melt -

chock full of

teary-eyed nights

and

learning to love these curls

look in the mirror and smile;

you made it.

in eyes brown and

       quiet sarcasm

          are the out-loud thoughts

of a woman in white and black and

who picked these colours anyway?

it's a long story,

      like self-histories we're made of

        in the memories our legacies carry
                    forward;

              life's great river

         collective unconscious

rolling deep on into cosmic reality.

Chains heavy, don't break easy,

      not without fire of heart and mind

              and spirit

        clamouring for forgiveness

when the only person to forgive

is yourself.

you,

the painted-monster maybe who makes
more than their fair share of mess;

power and beauty do not escape you

yet happiness generated without

has left you searching within

and brown eyes making me melt

pardon that broken heart mind-mangled
soul of mine

until passion consumes like fire

the heart that died the least

i miss a face and a voice and a
presence and the way her eyes seem to
sparkle.

huh,

 that's treasure buried in plain sight.

27

   i saw without rose lenses

took the glasses off slowly cause it was
too bright

  and you weren't there but

     i felt you;

somehow we've all been here

  stuck nowhere

 with someone lost in our minds

 because the truth is that we never catch
       them.

why would we?

love is made to be free.

8.collage in winter

how miraculous

      the sound of silence

amplifies the snows grasp

on my insides;

      churning,

drawn to comfortable nothingness.

      Perhaps it has answers for us.

Snow doesn't deserve to be as beautiful
    as it is (but you already know that).

Perhaps we lie to protect the ones we
        love.

I'm blinking in slow motion,

   clouds drop crystals onto

passersby,

the wind does it's thing (you know),

   eyes brace themselves to be

stung,

   hands prepare to be bitten,

     have you ever felt invisible?

i have. but not to myself.

     there, the sun beams

behind those grey clouds

   and

   someone said

we all have potential;

we all have potential.

We all have potential.

we all find our El Dorado.

If you're confused

as much as I am

to be this: human. being.

then you know

you know how mad this all is... we are
always busy Being™ and,

    as such,

we never stop to Abstract™.

    certainly,

    not enough.

I am, therefore I think,

    no.

I think, therefore I am.

To err is -

the hand smacked again,

a cliché rocking back and forth

on a rotted wooden porch.

I open the window

but the wind can't reach me

through the walls i've built.

       Still,

         itgets cold in here sometimes.

         and so,

I shrink from the window and return to
work.

         I return to snow.

I remember who lives inside these walls.

9.a fleeting star

i was away on a mission and i missed
your call

while my ship straddled the edge of the
cosmos -

the difference between the light and the
dark

opens up a universe of possibilities.

she smiles brightest when she's
dreamin' of the stars,

i smile brightest when i dream of her;

world's apart.

10.sublime

sublime

like telling you it's over

without uttering a single word

like bubbling lava

rising to the surface of a precipice,

our tears consume this Pompeii

we fought facing the reality

of what we aren't,

while embracing at last

a touch centuries denied

my mind traces our souls

and witnesses this decline

a fork in the road

becomes a knife

i bleed, you bleed

coagulating

we reminisce over the cause of death,

investigate the shadows

of a nuclear fallout.

nothing survives

but the dark imprints of the past,

they reveal our secrets,

expose every weakness.

fractured pieces of imperfect lives,

concrete albums lost in the
self-destruction,

written on the inside of our eyelids

while life sucks venom from deep
wounds.

in death, we embrace love.

in life, we embrace death.

.

11.Throwback thursday

blood runs dry

     like tears falling on a coral
sweater,

     freezing fabric to a warm chest,

beating feverishly

with a heart that threatens

to end itself;

screaming into a pillow,

you bite down on your emotions

but take a giant mouthful

of reality with you -

a sucker punch to the gut;

a cigarette put out on soft skin,

broken far too easily.

nicotine-stained nails

run under the kitchen tap,

the stained walls bleeding

into the air with sick.

the greatest lie we forget to tell
ourselves:

that dreams are only dreams

and

believing is seeing.

12.home

there were these

    stains

    like handprints

impressed upon concrete;

    void -

a reminiscence:

    memories

    made maddeningly murky.

    this house

so full it feels empty,

slipping down the drain

alongside remnants

like a closet Goodwill;

everything is lost,

everything is found,

trapped like

bitter thoughts

dying of yesterday's

laughter.

rebuild,

repair,

repaint,

a smile worn too often

eventually tears;

new wallpaper fixes

a temporary view;

you should never leave yourself

in your time of need.

i will gut you.

i will tear your skin

    strip by strip.

i will climb into your darkest recesses

to unearth your truth.

    and,

i will call you home.

13.a view through the trees

how these emotions twist

carefree as a sentimental kiss;

curled inwards and outwards,

the branches of time

reach everywhere and nowhere,

aimless... or free?

seen through eyes draped in shadows,

wintering at the thoughts

that hollow

the mind that mourns

and

the seeds never reaped nor sown

14.reflection

i came here to breathe...

whichi never understood

as a matter of privilege

until

i realized

i only have to look over my shoulder

half of the time

and

there's still a chance

a siren or flashing lights

aren't a death sentence -

a chance:

50/50.

the water

is rife with voices,

whispering woes

colonial violence wrought;

wrenching bodies

into narrow ideologies,

rending families,

goring humanity

and

cribbing countless corpses

for capital;

your guts have to be worth something

or

you're as good as

a knee on your neck

in broad daylight

                                    or

eight gunshots while you're in bed

or

a point blank playground tragedy... Like
the whipped flesh

on my ancestors back,

society splits open,

revealing truths long denied

but always apparent:

there is not yet justice.

there is not yet peace.

and

we are the change

that shall never cease.

15.For Mom

All of the flowers in the night's sky,

glistening by the crescent egg white,

would be mere fantasies

if you had not brought me into this
world.

My love for you is full of warmth;

slow-burning embers of a low campfire

refusing to die on a perfect summers
eve.

I will never be cold.

When I sing, your voice echoes through
mine.

How infinitesimal this existence would
be

if it were so without you.

16.yet to forget

night is irreversible

in a world where

all the lightswitches

are taped-over.

irreversible,

the emotional fabric

of our reality,

blossoming,

sweet, uncertain alchemy -

to taste the love on your lips

and feel it in your eyes

that haunt me in dreams,

love melting into

midnight musings

my arm around your shoulder

everything

except us

disintegrates

a paper straw melts

into a cup

and

it isn't enough to save any of us

because

love is the only way

17.braveheart

wildflowers and wanderlust,

hearts swiftly beating,

pulsing,

dancing

in deepest

pockets

of sunshine;

let me melt with you

in the light

like the yellow and white

meadows

meld with

the cold, clear blue,

and

everything,

including us,

feels

timeless.